Dressing
in the Dark

Clothes supplied by Bergdorf Goodman
Additional clothing from Peter Elliot and Hugo Boss
Photographs by Kanji Ishi
Styling by Luiz Antonio Machado

Page 4: James Garner and a roomful of suits.

© 2002 Assouline Publishing, Inc.
Assouline Publishing, Inc.
601 West 26th Street 18th Floor
New York, NY 10001, USA
Tel.: 212 989-6810   Fax: 212 647-0005

www.assouline.com

ISBN: 2 84323 361 5

Printed by Grafiche Milani (Italy)

Marion Maneker

Dressing
in the Dark

LESSONS IN MEN'S STYLE

FROM THE MOVIES

ASSOULINE

CONTENTS

Introduction

What's wrong with men? This is, no doubt, a question women have pondered for centuries. It also has been a persistent question in the fashion business. "What's wrong with men?" everyone from the designers to the retail clerks ask. Why can't they dress well? Why, when offered every opportunity to take some interest in their clothes, do men take a ludicrous pleasure in looking like drab carbon copies of the same ill-clad chump? Why can't they get their clothes to match? Why can't they show up properly dressed for a job interview, a dinner with a client, or a family barbecue?

Confronted with this question, most men let out a self-satisfied chuckle, assuming that the query does not apply to them. But ask a sophisticated woman why men don't dress well and she will tell you matter-of-factly that men lack imagination. This is exactly right, most men truly lack a sartorial imagination. And those who do possess one are branded with an almost contemptuous word: "dandy." It's as if caring about clothes makes a man something other than a man.

Today the problem of masculine attire has become even more pressing than usual. Why? Because in the last few years, men have borne the brunt of a sweeping cultural change. The introduction of computers, cell phones and the internet caused seismic shifts in work, that masculine redoubt. Barriers

66 In the 1990s, a new masculine ideal emerged: The road warrior and the 24-hour employee. 99

Ready, Steady, Go: Clark Gable relaxes on set, previous page. Right, Ben Affleck frets over what to wear.

between our public and private lives, which technology had been opening for years, suddenly collapsed, causing our work life and home life to merge and changing our expectations about codes of conduct—and attire—in both places.

In the 1990s, a new masculine ideal emerged: the road warrior and the 24-hour employee. If a job was worth doing, the new motto seemed to run, then it was worth doing all the time. Men found themselves in a variety of social settings that could no longer be categorized as either work or personal life. How does one dress when one lives at work? How to dress when one works at home? And what about all the spaces and places in between? The delicate irony of this social sea change cannot be overlooked. One of the least important aspects of a man's life, his clothes, changed the most during the technological revolution. Where men had once had a small vocabulary of clothes appropriate for work—suit, tie and solid colored shirt (white or blue)—they suddenly now had an uncomfortably wide array of clothes—virtually anything—to wear. To make matters worse, the new man had to dress comfortably for every role he was expected to play during a given day: working in the office, picking up the kids from school, or traveling across the country for a sales call or a conference.

However, instead of unleashing the pent-up creativity of men who had longed to get out their constricting blue suits, this newfound sartorial freedom created a work force of men clad in a uniform of khakis and polo shirts. Impetuous guys, celebrating the end of the suit-and-tie orthodoxy, threw out whole closets full of Armani and Hugo Boss. In response, stores rolled out racks of khakis, as if that could satisfy the thirst for a new way of getting dressed. What one didn't see in the stores, however, was a way of dressing that might combine the spirit behind a classic suit with the freshness and comfort of casual clothing. You didn't see new principles emerge that men could absorb and abide by. You didn't see anything that resembled a new orthodoxy.

Then all the social tumult ended. The New Economy deflated and some stability returned. But a funny thing happened: having tasted the freedom of casual dress, men didn't want to go back. Sure, there are more suits around today than a few years ago. But not that many more. Today, men still show up to work in dressed-down suits or dressed-up casual clothes. The men who can dress, or care to take it seriously, are having a field day choosing from the vast repertoire that one hundred years of men's fashion has left them.

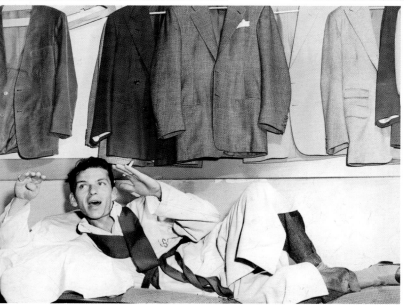

Above. Burt Reynolds shows that style is no small matter as he contemplates the perfect look. Frank Sinatra relaxes in a dressing gown while lying under his wardrobe at the Paramount in New York.

The great mass of men, however, has been left in a fix. The casual revolution isn't the only reason most men have lost their sartorial bearings. Most well-dressed men used to learn the basic principles of style from their fathers. Sure, every man had to achieve his independence—and develop a sartorial imagination—but men were introduced to the mysteries of suits and ties as a right of passage. Learning to tie a Windsor knot while encircled in a father's arms was once a milestone every bit as important to a man as his first drink. But now, the rules about how to dress have changed since our fathers' generation.

"Most men know more about their cars than they do about their clothes," fashion writer G. Bruce Boyer once complained. This comment will seem not only true to most men but also will be deemed the right allocation of brainpower. However, clothes and cars aren't as far apart as one might think: both are utilitarian aspects of men's lives that are ultimately judged as means of self-expression. Guys might be more familiar with (and forgiving of) the gearhead than with the dandy, but both are driven by the same masculine impulse to show off. As for why most men prefer horsepower to thread count, it's probably as much nurture as nature. Most high schools have a very popular class called Auto Shop; how many have a course in haberdashery?

Once he has grown up and discovered the power of clothes, a man may wish his school had offered Style 101 alongside Typing and Home Economics. But don't hold your breath waiting for one to appear on the local night school curriculum. Even now, as men getting dressed stare into the mirror to find a goggling expression of panic, clothes-sense seems exotic to the point of arousing suspicion. To care about the way you look appears to be a more shameful vice than having problems with drugs or alcohol. To most men, experimenting with the unsurpassed variety of clothes available today would be an act of exploration as bold as Shackleton's trip to Antarctica. The closet, it would seem, is the one place where a man's unspoken demons still lie.

It doesn't have to be this way. Sartorially, at least, we live in the best of times. Men have at their disposal well-made and eye-catching clothes from a brilliant array of contemporary designers and classic menswear manufacturers. Stores are literally full of exciting and wearable clothing, suits and

The Ties that Bind: Peter Lawford inspects his ties. The right choice can bring a suit to life, but the wrong one will ruin the whole effect.

ties as well as high-tech athletic gear that would easily fill out the wardrobe of a cultivated, successful man.

All men need is a little imagination, and some of that can be taught. The problem lies in their limited experience with clothes and minimum guidance in matters of style. No man feels comfortable asking his buddy, the way women readily do, "Do I look good in this?" Consequently, men avoid the give-and-take that constitutes learning. Lacking confidence in their judgment, men tend to shy away from risks. Unwilling to ask for help, they simply mimic what they see other men wear. Now, this isn't a problem—taking lessons from memorably well-dressed men is just about the best way to develop a style of one's own.

In their daily lives, men come across few other men who can actually give them a sense of how to express themselves through their clothes. What a man needs, more than anything, is a mentor, a guide, someone like his father—but maybe a little hipper. Where can a man find examples worth emulating? Hollywood, of course. Movies (which one can easily go out and rent) hold a detailed and accessible record of what some stylish and sophisticated men wore. Through a century of motion pictures we have a record of nearly every development in men's fashion, starting with the modern suit and ending with casual clothes.

Men's style evolved in the hot-house of a wealthy leisured group. The British aristocracy led the way by inventing or repurposing every major piece of the masculine wardrobe in the first half of the twentieth century. When you look back at the history of men's clothes you can see that there's really nothing tailors and designers haven't tried already once or twice (including casual dress based on the model of the suit).

For seventy years or more, Hollywood has been the one place in America where work and play, business and social life have been completely intertwined. Moreover, Hollywood is the sort of place where men make up their own sartorial rules. For example, they gave up on ties decades before the rest of the country. Years later, they led the change from English tailored clothing to Italian comfort clothes. And after pioneering the Armani suit-and-sneaker look, movie folks led the charge into Prada suits. Whether it was led by agents, directors, studio bosses or stars, every significant change in men's clothes has reached its apogee in Hollywood—from the elegance of the thirties and the dark, imposing forties through the stripped down conformity of the fifties and into the streamlined sixties, the flamboyant seventies, and so on.

Attitude is Everything: Jean-Paul Belmondo kicks back during the filming of Breathless, above. Even a half-dressed Belmondo exudes his character's signature nonchalant style. Below, Sammy Davis, Jr. struts his stuff on a runway, his sleek turtleneck and slim trousers giving his casual look a composed formality.

But don't look to the movies for an all-purpose answer to your style questions. One cannot simply find a formula to being well dressed. Certainly, no one can prescribe the right way to dress. That's not what style is about. But one can learn to look at movies and to pay attention to what the men wear in specific situations. From there one can derive some basic sartorial principles.

To start with, any movie with Fred Astaire, Gary Cooper or Cary Grant will immediately improve one's style intelligence. Jeremy Irons and Jude Law have a natural presence that melds with their clothes, but the clothes also are worth paying attention to. Robert Downey, Jr., Steve McQueen, Al Pacino, John Travolta and Sean Penn all light up a movie screen. One of their tools to get into character is choosing the right wardrobe. So, the lesson of this book is while watching movies to pay less attention to the acting and more to the way the clothes express character. Once a man masters this habit, he can apply it around town, at work or out on the town.

If this book can accomplish one thing it will be to give men ideas. There is no one way to dress well, especially in these eclectic times, but there are many ways to dress badly. With a little guidance, and the help of a few dozen movies, most men should be able to learn to get dressed in the morning with a little imagination.

Gun Shy: Warren Beatty played the clothes-obsessed gangster Bugsy Siegel in Bugsy. Walking on the back lot, Beatty shows the simple power of a well-cut grey suit.

The King, McQueen: Steve McQueen is the patron saint of our casual era. Combining an offbeat sense of humor with a naturally understated style, McQueen captures the spirit of men's fashion today whether he's mocking formality, left, or toeing his marks, right.

Never Let Them See You Sweat: Fred Astaire is
the original movie star as fashion icon. His greatest contribution to masculine style is the ever-
present reminder that you should look comfortable and relaxed in your clothes. Here he prac-
tices a dance routine in a polo shirt and flannel
pants. Instead of a belt, he wears a silk scarf
knotted around his waist. The absence of belt
loops makes it easier to move while dancing (the
silk in the scarf functions like a shock absorber).

Suits of Armor

"Do you know that scene in The Thomas Crown Affair," Frank Rostron, a British shirt maker once confided to me, "the one where Steve McQueen's wearing a beautiful Prince of Wales checked suit with a powder blue shirt and a royal blue tie?" Once I'd confirmed that I too appreciated the importance of that moment in film history, the tailor rolled his eyes back slightly, his lids hooding to help him savor the memory. "Seeing that," he went on, "made me want to become a tailor."

Just Suit Me: The original Thomas Crown Affair, previous page, remains one of the best movies for learning how to wear a suit and tie. Steve McQueen's pale blue shirt, royal blue tie and classic three-piece Prince of Wales suit conveys his character's old-money background and reckless thrill seeking better than any dialogue. In Goodfellas, above, the gangsters' outlandish characters are captured in their fixation with telling details such as the pronounced long collar points.

If you're like most men, you find it hard to love a suit. Maybe you remember buying one for your first job interview and now associate it with all that disapproving bombast. A suit seems to represent all that's confining and constraining in the world, like the oppressively hierarchical office, where you are judged not by style points but merely for fitting in.

Such an environment hardly shows the suit to its best advantage. Want to see a man dressed for work who's dressed for battle? Look at a movie like *Wall Street*, where designer Alan Flusser gave Michael Douglas the look of a larger-than-life corporate raider by dressing him in softly tailored conservative suits. It helped to add distinctive touches like horizontally striped shirts and other subtle but bold touches. In that movie, Michael Douglas epitomizes the use of a perfectly tailored suit to establish rank. More than his limousines and beach house, Flusser's suits separate corporate raider Gordon Gekko from those around him. Gekko's magnetism, amplified by his clothes, drives the entire movie.

The same is true in the original *Thomas Crown Affair*. Steve McQueen wears a series of spectacular three-piece suits (with shirts and ties in striking complementary colors) that establish him as both a wealthy Boston wasp and a self-made iconoclast bored with the conventional life he's obtained.

Wearing a suit, however, doesn't have to restrict you to office work. Tom Cruise opened up a new way of dressing in *Rain Man* by wearing a grey suit with a white shirt (his shirt collar provocatively buttoned to the top) and no tie. The simplicity of his clothes fitted his character's self-confidence. He was, after all, playing a slick Ferrari salesman. But they also marked him as a self-assured man who kept his own counsel.

Don't forget that gangsters, the very definition of men who need to be judged on their appearances, have always loved suits. And no one has ever accused them of lacking spirit. Edward G. Robinson's tight suits in *Little Caesar* show what a jumped-up tough guy can look like (though John Leguizamo in *Carlito's Way* wins the prize for best aspiring thug.) The goombas of *Goodfellas* wearing their suits with those strikingly inappropriate closed collar points will live forever in your imagination. You'll never dress that way, but it's nice to know that someone did.

If you still can't picture yourself in a suit, try to remember that in *Saturday Night Fever*, John Travolta's Tony Manero (who never saw the inside of an office in his entire life) pretty much changed the world in a white three-piece suit and black open-necked shirt.

These few examples should go a long way toward explaining why the suit remains the building block of any man's wardrobe. If you choose the right one, a suit is flexible and shockingly useful. There are men who will leave for a week-long business trip having packed only shirts, shoes and ties—confident that they can appear comfortably and appropriately dressed wearing the same dark suit one day with a sweater, the next with braces and a tie. You can split up the pants and coat, substituting a raincoat or quilted shell.

Slick Ahoy: Gary Cooper sets sail in a suit.

The Front-runner: Sometimes what distinguishes a man is not the stylishness of his clothes but the manner in which he conveys his sincerity. Robert Redford in The Candidate, above, mutes his spectacular good looks with an understated suit. Clark Gable, right, demonstrates that an elegant suit need not be bright or complicated.

Of course, to get that sort of utility out of a suit, it has to be subtle and rely more on detail than flat-out flash. What you see again and again in the movies are suits that strike a single note—authoritative pin stripes or a versatile Glen plaid—that can then be incorporated into a variety of uses. Part of the trick is developing a repertoire of clothes appropriate to your personality. Then mixing them up to suit your mood.

The first step is finding one or two manufacturers whose clothes appeal to you and your sense of self. For conservative tastes, there's Brooks Brothers; Polo; Hickey-Freeman; Kilgour, French and Stanbury; Paul Stuart; Chester

Barrie; and Oxford. All make some version of the loose-fitted, natural-shouldered look without too much flash. In the stylistic middle, you get Italian names like Zegna, Isaia, Belvest, Corneliani, Cerrutti, Battistoni, and Luciano Barbera, whose suits possess the structured nonchalance Italians are famous for with small variations that accommodate personal style. Finally, if you're bold enough to carry it off, there are the unmistakable silhouettes of Ralph Lauren Purple Label (selective takes on Savile Row classics), Giorgio Armani (the master of the slouching power look), Kiton (Neapolitan flash), Huntsman (British military precision) and Brioni (Roman cool).

Once you've found a manufacturer you're comfortable with, you should look for two or three styles that are becoming to your frame, face and situation in life. Not everyone looks good in a double-breasted suit, and there are plenty of places where too much tailoring will make you look like a gigolo. Whatever models you settle upon, take the time to develop a personal style. Instead of

buying suits all in one go during your triennial trip to the department store, try to acquire a suit or two at a time. Live with it; wear it; then, decide what you'd like next. And if you're worried about the changing seasons or a designer's moods, ask if your favorite suit maker has a made-to-measure program where you get to choose your fabrics and details no matter what the current vogue happens to be.

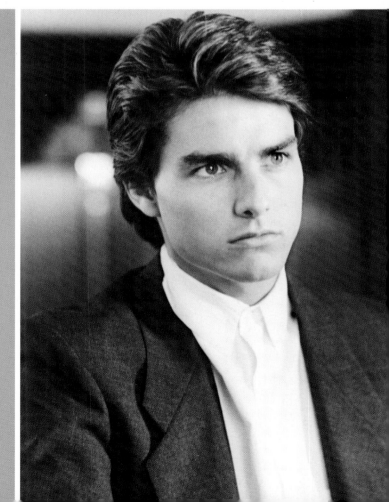

Good and Greedy: Michael Douglas personified power dressing in Wall Street, left, with his contrast-collared shirt and boldly coordinated tie and braces combination. But power dressing remains a rarified pursuit. At nearly the same time, Tom Cruise, right, knocked some of the starch out of suits by appearing in Rain Man as a fast-talking salesman who wore a white shirt with no tie.

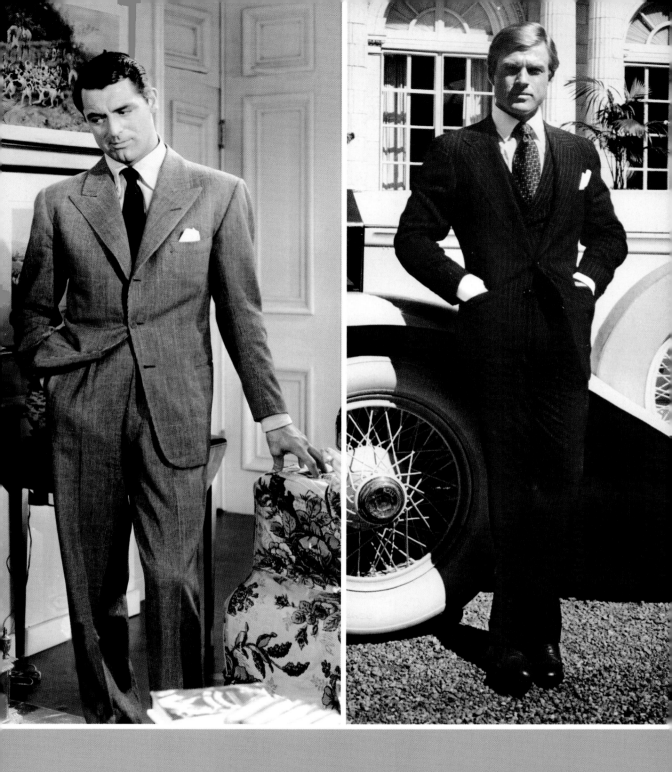

Four Square: These four photos explain the lounge suit's longevity as the bulwark of men's clothing. Each star wears a suit in his own way. Cary Grant, far left, is wearing a three-button sack suit, a classic American style, in The Philadelphia Story. Robert Redford, near left, plays Jay Gatsby, a self-made man with a sense of style, in a three-piece drape suit. Mick Jagger, right, shows off Savile Row's hip sixties persona in a tight-trousered mod suit. Fred Astaire, far right, exemplifies the subtle detail of timeless style in a double-breasted pin-stripe suit.

MEN OF IRON:

SUITS SHOULD BE THE MOST EXPENSIVE ITEMS IN YOUR WARDROBE. THEY'RE A MAJOR PURCHASE. SO MAKE SURE YOU GET A SUIT THAT'S BUILT TO LAST. IT SHOULD BE SOLIDLY CONSTRUCTED AND STYLED IN A TIMELESS WAY AND IN A COLOR THAT YOU WON'T GROW TIRED OF. THAT'S WHY SO MANY MEN'S SUITS ARE BLUE OR GREY (BROWN USED TO BE A STAPLE COLOR BUT HAS SOMEHOW FALLEN OUT OF FAVOR) AND COME IN CLASSIC PATTERNS LIKE PIN STRIPES OR NAILHEADS.

Cooper's Super: Bill Blass called Gary Cooper, previous page, the man "every man wanted to look like." Cooper's great size and sartorial restraint make him the ideal all men should aspire to, but don't forget that he was willing to wear strong patterns. A classic look such as pin stripes, opposite, should be in every man's wardrobe, especially when paired with a muted blue shirt to highlight the blue in the suit and lush rose-colored tie for smartness and contrast.

Pack Rats: Too bad you didn't hang on to your father's thin-lapeled suits from the sixties. The cocktail-culture style has become a classic for hipsters everywhere, not just Peter Lawford, Dean Martin, Sammy Davis, Jr. and Frank Sinatra.

THE DEVIL'S IN THE DETAILS:

FOLLOWING THIS ADVICE, WELL-DRESSED MEN USE THE TINY DETAILS OF A SUIT TO EXPRESS INDIVIDUALITY AND A SENSE OF HUMOR. POCKETS CAN COME WITH FLAPS OR SIMPLE JETS. PANTS CAN COME WITH PLAIN FRONTS OR PLEATS GOING EITHER DIRECTION (IN OR OUT.) TICKET POCKETS, THOSE EXTRA POCKETS HIGH ON THE RIGHT SIDE OF A JACKET, ARE A WELCOME NOVELTY (AND GREAT FOR CELL PHONES.) VENTS CAN COME IN THE CENTER, ON THE SIDES, OFFSET, OR NOT EXIST AT ALL. MOST OF ALL, YOU CAN WEAR A SUIT WITH A ONE-, TWO-, OR THREE-BUTTON STANCE, DOUBLE-BREASTED OR SINGLE, PEAK LAPELS OR NOTCHED. AND NONE OF THESE CHOICES SERIOUSLY FOLLOWS FASHION.

CHOOSE OR LOSE:

GIVEN ALL THESE OPTIONS, A MAN SHOULD REALLY KNOW WHAT SUITS HIM BEST. YOU NEEDN'T CONFINE YOURSELF TO ONE STYLE OF SUIT, DOUBLE-BREASTED OR SINGLE, BUT YOU SHOULD HAVE A SENSE OF WHAT LOOKS GOOD ON YOU AND TRY TO ACQUIRE SUITS IN THAT STYLE. ONCE A MAN'S GOT A SENSE OF HIMSELF, HE'S HALFWAY DOWN THE ROAD TO GETTING A SENSE OF STYLE.

The Monkey Suit

Just about every man looks better in a tuxedo. You don't have to be James Bond or even Brad Pitt. Just take a look at Anthony Hopkins in Meet Joe Black. The old guy really keeps up his end. This may be due simply to the high contrast of formal wear—black and white's outward simplicity is elegant beyond improvement.

" The tuxedo is the only part of a man's wardrobe that lets him indulge in the rococo aspects of dressing like a man: When else can you wear something as silly as a cummerbund? "

The casual atmosphere at the office these days only has increased our appetite for party clothes. Even guys who don't button their top button at work enjoy a special occasion now and then. The tuxedo is the only part of a man's wardrobe that lets him indulge in the rococo aspects of dressing like a man: When else can you wear something as silly as a cummerbund?

A tuxedo says, "I've come to spend the evening with you, and I would look inappropriate anyplace else right now." It's an outfit that makes you feel different, above the usual rule of having to get home early so you can get up in the morning. That's why it's considered formal wear. But beware, true formal wear is white tie and a tail coat. The sort of

These Little Town Blues: Frank Sinatra strikes a louche, up-all-night pose. When getting dressed in a tuxedo, every man has a little inkling that he might just go out until dawn, Sinatra-style.

Vested Interest: The formal vest has been losing a lot of ground over the last few years. Don't let this classic die. Steve McQueen's Thomas Crown knew how to look cool in a vest and you can too. Just don't follow the Brits in the silly fad for "fancy" vests, those bright concoctions meant to give a tuxedo "personality." Much better to choose the current vogue for four-in-hand ties paired with black, white or grey vests. When done right, this new look combines the best of the old and the new.

RENT TO OWN:

TUXEDOS ARE JUST LIKE ANYTHING ELSE, IF YOU BUY ONE YOU'LL HAVE MORE USE FOR IT THAN IF YOU ALWAYS HAVE TO RENT ONE TO GO TO SOME FORMAL EVENT. IN TODAY'S DRESS-DOWN WORLD, THERE SEEM TO BE MORE AND MORE BLACK TIE EVENTS THAT GIVE PEOPLE THE FEELING OF HAVING A SPECIAL NIGHT OUT. SO, IF YOU'RE AT ALL SERIOUS ABOUT YOUR CLOTHES, IT'S PROBABLY TIME TO BUY YOUR OWN TUX.

NOTCH ON YOUR LIFE:

THE MOST DISTURBING TREND IN TUXEDOS IS THE WIDESPREAD USE OF NOTCH LAPEL JACKETS INSTEAD OF THE TRADITIONAL SHAWL OR PEAK COLLAR. GUYS WHO RARELY WEAR SUITS MIGHT NOT NOTICE THE DIFFERENCE, BUT THERE'S A WORLD OF STYLE DIFFERENCE BETWEEN TACKING SOME SATIN ONTO A BLACK SUIT AND REALLY WEARING A TUXEDO. SINCE YOU'RE NEVER GOING TO WEAR A SHAWL COLLAR SUIT, INDULGE YOURSELF WHEN YOU BUY THAT TUXEDO.

THE VELVET REVOLUTION:

DON'T FORGET THAT THE TUXEDO WAS ORIGINALLY DESIGNED FOR DINNER PARTIES AT HOME, SO IT'S NO WONDER THAT LOTS OF MEN WEAR VELVET SMOKING JACKETS IN BURGUNDY, BLUE OR GREEN INSTEAD OF THE STANDARD DINNER JACKET. ONCE YOU'VE BROKEN THE MOLD LIKE THAT, YOU'LL FIND COUNTLESS WAYS TO INNOVATE. SOME TAILORS HAVE MADE ELEGANT CORDUROY DINNER JACKETS, AND DESIGNERS HAVE DONE BEAUTIFUL THINGS WITH SILK AND QUILTING. THE POINT, IN THE END, IS TO WEAR SOMETHING LUSH AND LUXURIOUS. MAKE IT SOMETHING SPECIAL!

Previous pages, tuxedos are all about getting the details right. The pants must have a grosgrain stripe down the seams. The tuxedo is meant to approximate the military man's attire, so you need that stripe to complete the look (otherwise, you're just wearing a black suit). Invest in a pair of patent leather shoes, they really make a tuxedo sing. Finally, when you really feel that you're ready, get a nice white silk scarf to go the extra mile.

King's Ransom: You have to figure they came up with the term "natty" just for Nat "King" Cole and his influence on men's fashion. Cole exemplified the pared-down style of the fifties and sixties, and nowhere is this more evident than in his formal clothes.

Getting Casual

Long before an idea called "office casual" was ever uttered, Hollywood players were showing up for work without ties. In sunny Southern California, stars like Clark Gable showed up at the studio neatly dressed in a blue blazer and grey flannels. He could look neat and businesslike without having to wear a stuffy suit.

The Birth of Cool: Office casual clothes started as casual wear for a dressier era. Somehow, the look always brings Italian fashion to mind. Marcello Mastroianni just about invented it in La Dolce Vita, previous page. Jude Law and Matt Damon, left, give a study in contrasts in The Talented Mr. Ripley (if you're daring enough to emulate Jude Law at the office, at least throw on some socks). Mickey Rourke gives the look a little rough and tumble, right.

Frankly, I Don't Give a Damn: following page, Clark Gable shows off the ideal office casual clothes, a classic combination of blue blazer and grey flannel pants over a white shirt, following pages. These are go-anywhere clothes that you'll never have to apologize for.

Old Hollywood did it well. But the masters of this kind of self-assured dressing are the Italians. Look at Marcello Mastroianni in *La Dolce Vita*. Affecting a sense of indifference, Mastroianni never looks out of place—but also never looks like he's trying too hard. It's an attitude Jude Law copies in *The Talented Mr. Ripley*. His vacation clothes have a neat nonchalance that expresses his charisma—and the kind of self-assurance that comes with great wealth. One can easily imagine him at a client meeting if he weren't cruising the Italian riviera.

The lesson you want to draw from this is simple: It's not about casual, it's about comfort. The impression you want to give with a casual wardrobe is that you are comfortable in your clothes and comfortable with your job. So comfortable, in fact, that you don't need some silly suit to show that you are a serious player (think David Geffen, pre-DreamWorks).

Unfortunately, men crave uniforms and feel overwhelmed by too many choices. The trick of the moment is to find a uniform that fits your work while still achieving the twin goals of being comfortable and projecting authority and accomplishment.

Whether it's a suit or a suede jacket, the new work wardrobe is built around a well-made and distinctive jacket. A jacket establishes who you are and what you do. For example, in an earlier era, writers were immediately recognizable by their nubbly tweed jackets and knit ties. Today, creative

The impression you want to give with a casual wardrobe is that you are comfortable in your clothes and comfortable with your job. So comfortable, in fact, that you don't need some silly suit to show that you are a serious player.

people in advertising and television are as likely to wear an expensive anorak to work as they are a sports jacket. The impulse is a valid one. Sporting clothes have always been a major element of a man's work wardrobe. The original office casual uniform was something a man might wear on Fridays before heading out to the country for a weekend. Just before the weekend, stuffy offices used to be filled with men in jackets and ties but not suits. (Remember, this was an era when men actually wore ties on the weekend, even while they were playing sports.)

Showing up at the office in riding clothes was one way to say that you're successful enough to spend your weekends on a horse farm. Perhaps that's why so many men in Hollywood used to walk around in jodhpurs. Today, you're more likely to spend a weekend mountain biking or hiking in the hills. While you wouldn't want to come into work dressed like you're making an assault on Mt. McKinley, you might wear some of that expensive North Face gear to work on Friday just so your office mates will wonder if you're spending the weekend doing practice climbs.

But dressing like you've got better things to do isn't the only way to show that you're comfortable in your professional role. An alternative work uniform is slowly emerging for men who think wearing a sport jacket and tie is both too casual and too constraining, but still don't feel they need to wear

California Dreaming: Michael Douglas first made his name, as both an actor and a dresser, on The Streets of San Francisco. A comfortable corduroy jacket and plaid shirt will get you through a casual Friday and into the weekend.

a tie. Recently, more and more men have been coming to work in a dark suit and colorful open-neck shirt. One New York shirtmaker calls this style of dressing "the powershirt" because bright stripes or checks become the same distinctive focal point that the power tie once was.

Although you can easily recycle your power suits for this style of dressing, it does work better with a three-button single-breasted suit. You might wear a patch-pocket coat instead of a more formal suit jacket to add to the casual feel.

This outfit has the added benefit of being familiar to many men, so it functions as a uniform without feeling constricting. Since there is a fairly restricted vocabulary of shirt patterns, the number of choices is limited but the selection of colors offers an outlet for personality and creativity. Finally, by keeping a couple of ties within reach, the man who goes to work dressed this way can always upgrade if a client drops by or the boss has a surprise opening in the corporate dining room.

Where can one get distinctive patterned shirts? You can get a better shirt that will last longer for just a little more money if you go to a custom shop. Many men extol the virtues of bespoke shirts by praising the superior cut, the higher-quality construction, or the ample choice of collar styles and cuff treatments. While all of these rationales hold water, the best thing about having your shirts made is the freedom to pick the patterns and colors you want, in the season in which you want them.

Finally, if shirts just aren't your thing, take a lesson from Robert Redford in *The Sting*. A bold suit with a simple white shirt will cover all the bases. You'll look successful because of the suit, and the white shirt will show that you don't have to scream for attention. What better way to prove you're comfortable than never having to raise your voice?

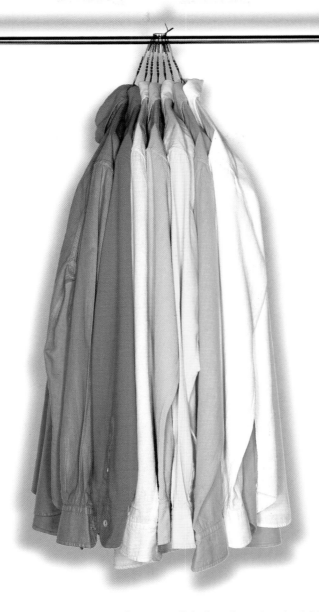

Hue and Cry: Colorful shirts will make any suit seem a little less formal and a lot less stuffy. The perfect wardrobe contains a serious array of bright colors and patterns. In the casual era, men don't wear power ties—they wear power shirts.

THEY CALL THEM CASUALTIES:

WHATEVER THEY SAY ABOUT THE NEW REALITIES OF WORK, FORMAL DRESSING IS NEVER COMING BACK. HOWEVER, DRESSING DOWN ISN'T AN EXCUSE FOR DRESSING CARELESSLY. IN FACT, CASUAL DRESSING, WITH ITS LACK OF CODES AND BROADER COLOR PALETTE, IS HARDER TO PULL OFF THAN GETTING SUITED UP FOR WORK. SO, IF YOU'RE GOING TO BE A CASUAL GUY, YOU STILL HAVE TO DRESS LIKE YOU MEAN IT.

REPEAT THE PAST:

THE GOLDEN AGE OF CASUAL DRESSING OCCURRED IN HOLLYWOOD IN THE TWENTIES AND THIRTIES WHEN MEN WORE AN IMPRESSIVE ARRAY OF CLOTHES INSPIRED BY SPORTS AND LEISURE ACTIVITIES. OUR CASUAL ERA WOULD BE MUCH BETTER SERVED IF MEN COPIED NORFOLK JACKETS, JODHPURS, COATS WITH BI-SWING BACKS OR EVEN NEHRU JACKETS.

The New Rules: A casual uniform, previous page, has emerged since the demise of the dress codes. It consists of a dark suit and bold shirt. Dandier men will want to accessorize with a pocket square—call it the new power tie. Rough shoes like these Norwegians, combined with striking shirts, will make your conservative suits more casual.

George Clooney and Brad Pitt take a meeting in Ocean's Eleven, left.

Working for the Weekend

If there's a sartorial danger zone in contemporary life, it has to be the weekend. With work and play collapsing into one category, the weekend seems to have become an excuse for wandering around in your underwear.

Softwear: Having style on the weekend doesn't have to be like studying for an exam. Steve McQueen takes Fay Dunaway for a spin in his dune buggy in The Thomas Crown Affair, previous page. His clothes are vivid and stylish with out being complicated or fussy.

It's a style of dressing that Cary Grant captured in To Catch a Thief. Set on the French Riviera, Grant makes the most of sweaters and the occasional scarf.

66 While the rest of the week is laden with duties and responsibilities, the weekend should give you free reign to indulge your inner James Bond. 99

Clothes originally designed for sports or the gym, fleeces and nylon warm-up pants to mention only a few, appear all over town during the weekends. We kid ourselves into thinking that we're just running out early in the morning to do an errand or that we're truly on our way to the gym later in the day, but the truth of the matter is that we're walking around in public wearing clothes that were meant for private pursuits.

The trend toward an undifferentiated weekend attire has done the most damage to the restaurant business where men are unwilling to shed their T-shirts to sit down to a Saturday night meal. Most restaurants have abandoned their jacket-and-tie policies but are unable to define a dress code beyond "No Shirt. No Shoes. No Service." Like traveling, a facet of life where people used to wear their very best clothes, the weekend has become some sort of in-between time where comfort overrides formality or good taste.

The problem isn't about how to look good in gym togs. There are certainly a lot of wonderful workout clothes available. Rather, the problem is thinking about the weekend as a time with an appropriate dress code. While the rest of the week is laden with duties and responsibilities, the weekend should give you free reign to indulge your inner James Bond. To the rest of the world you may look like a neatly dressed man in a polo shirt and matching pants, but in your own mind you'd be on a Caribbean beach in search of Dr. No's hidden fortress.

Boys will be boys: Kirk Douglas relaxes in the sand, left, wearing an amalgam of costumes and comfortable clothes. Note the English riding boots and Western hat all combined with a comfortable cardigan. Douglas finds a distinctive style even while breaking all the rules.

David Soul and Paul Michael Glaser, right, were style leaders of the seventies on Starsky and Hutch, a cop show that was really a guide to the buddy life. Their clothes prove that men dress more for other guys than to impress women.

In reality, the weekends are for indulging in our passions. Steve McQueen was an obsessive car racer, a pursuit that found its fullest expression in the movie *Bullitt* where McQueen ostentatiously did much of his own driving. The movie was just an excuse to race down the streets of San Francisco going full tilt and not having to worry about Johnny Law. If you have an ounce of self-knowledge you'll admit that you would love to do that too.

For the unchallenged masterwork of casual dressing, you should rent *To Catch a Thief*, the Cary Grant movie. If you've seen it before, you probably spent the whole movie drooling over Grace Kelly. But this time you might want to pay closer attention to Cary Grant's clothes, especially in the scenes at his villa. Grant sashays through the movie in a palette of dark greys and blacks with a richly textured combination of tricot sweaters and flannel pants that almost scream comfort without making him look at all slovenly. The choice of subtle stripes or the addition of a red handkerchief loosely knotted under the crew-neck collar of a dark shirt adds color to these restrained outfits.

Flights of Fancy: packing for a weekend away shouldn't require a steamer trunk. Try to choose clothes that go together well. Sometimes that means neutrals, like these white pants, and strong but versatile accent pieces like this suede jacket and brown suede shoes. Add a colorful sweater vest and a few shirts and you'll have clothes that will take you from day into evening without breaking a sweat.

Sweatermen: Robert Taylor, above, was one of Hollywood's most masculine clothes horses. His look always had a hint of menace about it. But this cable-knit sweater brings out his benevolent side.

Clark Gable, right, cuddles up with a cardigan over a turtleneck sweater.

Texture is Everything: You can choose your sweaters for their color but you also need to pay attention to the gauge of the wool and knitting. Your closet should be filled with everything from rough woolens to creamy cashmeres. The outfit opposite mixes textures by combining a cashmere turtleneck with a woolen pair of pants.

Swinger: Steve McQueen proves there's life beyond golf shirts and saddle shoes for guys who want to look good while playing their favorite sports.

Opposite: Clothier Peter Elliot invented a denim blazer for those early morning errands. A simple addition to the usual outfit of sweatpants and sneakers, Peter Elliot's New York Times jacket lets the sophisticated weekender run out for the Sunday paper without having to get "dressed."

SPORTS

The history of men's fashion has followed a fairly simple trajectory: innovative new sports give birth to new clothes. These clothes become fashionable with people who want to look like aficionados, and, next thing you know, everyone's forgotten that the original purpose of the clothing was for sports.

Tweed jackets were originally made for hunting expeditions, their heavy fabric provided ideal warmth and protection from thorns while out tramping through the brush. Camel overcoats were first used by polo players to keep warm in between chukkers and, well, no one needs a lesson in how few men who own motorcycle jackets actually ride one. From boat moccasins to ski parkas, it's hard to think what men would be wearing if sporting gear hadn't been incorporated into our everyday life.

That influence doesn't have to go in only one direction. Sports are one of the public pursuits that could do with a little more attention to sartorial detail, because, unfortunately, not everyone has Steve McQueen's straightforward sense of style. You

see him here playing golf but dressed like he could go anywhere.

Robert Redford did much the same with ski clothes in the movie *Downhill Racer*. Ski sweaters have become nearly ubiquitous winter clothing for men who have never been on the slopes, and a whole new generation of fabrics are being employed in winter clothing. Some of those are made in such strikingly colorful designs that they make excellent fashion statements whether or not they function as insulation.

The point of this extended meditation on sports is that one's sense of style need not be abandoned just because one needs specialized clothing. There is, and needs to be, a way to dress for one's hobbies that either sets you apart from the crowd or, at the bare minimum, ensures that you look presentable.

A Theme Runs Through It: Sports have always been the incubator of men's fashion. Most men's clothes, even the suit, trace their origins to sporting life. So don't think of your weekend as time off, but as a laboratory of style.

We're Having a Party

What do Brad Pitt and Fight Club have to do with parties? Pitt certainly looks cool in a bold print shirt and a leather jacket. In fact, he's a masculine fantasy of the kind of guy every guy wants to emulate: confident, iconoclastic, and brutally tough. Throughout the movie, Pitt displays an insouciant magnetism highlighted by his rock star-like clothes. In that movie, Pitt is the sort of guy you'd pick out of a crowd. He's the most intriguing man at the party.

Shout: John Travolta lights up Grease's prom with this electric party outfit, previous page. You don't have to go for hot pink to make an outrageous statement when you're going out. A well-chosen pair of aggressive pants will do the trick just fine.

“ When you get dressed to go to a party, you're really getting outfitted for battle. ”

No good party is lacking in a certain element of danger. The ideal party has a frisson of excitement, the possibility that things might spiral out of control. Musicals like *Grease* play off this danger in a silly way by converting the danger into song and dance. A darker version of this same process is the party in *West Side Story* where a dance becomes a competition between the two gangs—and eventually a full-scale war.

A great party brings together many people who would not normally come into contact. After all, you get excited about parties and look forward to going to them because you're interested in meeting new and exotic people. What's the first question you ask about a party you missed?: "Who was there?" But with that excitement comes the potential for competition and combustion. When men come into contact with rivals and strangers—especially when the attention of women is at stake—they need to take extra care with the first impressions that they make. In other words, their clothes become exceptionally important. When you get dressed to go to a party, you're really getting outfitted for battle.

In one way or another, all the clothes that men wear today are originally derived from military uniforms. Uniforms combine elements of intimidation and display that deviate only very slightly from primitive displays of machismo. No scene in a movie illustrates this better than the climactic battle in *Braveheart*. Mel Gibson rides around on horseback with his face painted a frightening blue, giving a noble speech about freedom. But

Pulp Power: John Travolta in quintessential party mode in Pulp Fiction.

Fight Cub: Brad Pitt is full of piss and vinegar as every shy man's ideal alter ego in Fight Club. When you're at a party, bold prints and leather always help make a statement. Just be sure that you want to attract the kind of woman who likes dangerous guys. A tie tones down these pants, above, and gives you a little bit of a what-are-you-staring-at attitude about your in-your-face clothes.

Dean Martini: Getting through a bender isn't all about style but Dean Martin proves that a sense of fashion still helps. For an even better example, check out Jackie Gleason's Minnesota Fats in The Hustler: after a twenty-four hour game and a quart of booze, he's as fresh as a daisy with a perky flower in his lapel.

much of the battle is also preceded by a lengthy bout of taunts between the Scots and the English. These taunts are as purely masculine as one can imagine: the Scots raise the fronts of their kilts and expose themselves. Whatever the Scots are fighting for, the battle comes down to one thing: Who's bigger.

In the modern era, no one is going to go around raising his kilt to scare off a rival—or paint his face blue, for that matter—but that doesn't mean our battle dress is really much different. Getting dressed for a party may be one of the most important acts of social presentation available to a man. Women dress to show off their personal and physical attributes. Women at parties tend to be judged by their sex appeal, while men are judged more by their accomplishments than their physiques (how many times do you have to see a beautiful woman hanging on the arm of a rich, powerful or famous man to accept this?).

This quandary about self-presentation may help explain the famous scene in *American Gigolo* where Richard Gere lays out half of his Armani wardrobe on the bed searching for the combination of clothes. For a man who professionally services women, choosing the right clothes is even more fraught. When you think about it, Gere wasn't dressing to please his clients, the middle-aged ladies who paid for his services. Instead, he was dressing to convince the rest of the world that he was a legitimate suitor, a worthy man.

Which brings us to the practical question about how you should dress to go to a party. Think about who you are, then try to accentuate the basic aspect of your personality. If you're bookish, look smart. If you're cultured, look sophisticated. If you're strong, look confident. Party clothes allow for higher contrast and more cartoonish gestures. When you're going out, break out the pin stripes or the bright colors. Use your bold prints to make a point about your self-assurance. But whatever you do, don't start a fight.

Cherchez la Femme: Tony Curtis fends off an obvious play for his girl.

Elvis, left, always knew how to have a good time.

I'm Not Waiting on a Lady, I'm Just Waiting on a Friend: Mick Jagger and Keith Richards, opposite, raging in their party finery.

Tough Guys

With all our pumped-up action heroes teaching the world a lesson as one-man armies, you would think the memorable movie tough guys would be hulking men. But the steely characters who stick with us tend not to be brawny, imposing men like Victor Mature, Sylvester Stallone or James Gandolfini. Rather, it's the men of implacable will and slight frames, such as James Cagney and Humphrey Bogart, who really impress us with their personal magnetism.

The Delinquent Problem: Rebellious young men have favored leather jackets for more than fifty years. Alain Delon, previous page, gives a defiant stare. Marlon Brando was the epitome of macho cool in The Wild Ones, left, until his look was co-opted by the gay leather bar look.

Dennis Hopper, yes that's him on the stairs next to James Dean, played one of the original movie juvenile delinquents, right, complete with black leather jacket.

Think of Steve McQueen outwitting the Germans in *The Great Escape*—or just outlasting them by cheerfully taking his baseball glove and ball into solitary confinement after yet another failed breakout. Or Sean Penn's deceptively loopy Jeff Spicoli in *Fast Times at Ridgemont High*. Penn's stoner nonchalance is just the soft exterior of an obdurate survivor.

The greatest depiction of this sort of zen toughness has got to be Paul Newman's *Cool Hand Luke*. The clothes don't seem like much because he's on a prison chain gang, but they perfectly express Newman's ability to transform something humble and unassuming into undeniable power. Or, as the man-mountain George Kennedy says after he's been defeated in the big fight scene, "You kept coming back at me with nothing."

James Dean's *Rebel Without a Cause* is possibly the pivotal moment in the evolution of the savvy street-wise survivor. And it's no accident that he made blue jeans a style icon in that movie. The simplicity of his white T-shirt and jeans mirrors the movie's whole theme of a troubled young man unwilling to back down from a fight. Indeed, the entire plot of the movie is set in motion when Dean is taunted by a gang leader. He tries to avoid a fight, going as far as putting down his switchblade and walking away. But he can't leave once he's been called "chicken."

Marlon Brando's motorcycle gang leader in *The Wild Ones*, a character who seems not very threatening today, made jeans and leather a classic combination. Jeans and leather have become a universal ensemble, but the military-style cap has become a gay signifier in the nearly fifty intervening years since the movie was made.

Though street style has become much more influenced by hip-hop culture in recent years, it still works on the same vocabulary of leather and denim. It's the motorcycle look that's proved so lasting (even if few men will ever ride one). Peter Fonda in *Easy Rider* did more than anyone to popularize this look. (Dennis Hopper deserves some mention here because, although he didn't wear a leather jacket in *Easy Rider*, he is one of the leather jacket- and jeans-wearing tough guys in *Rebel Without a Cause*.) The Captain America chopper has gotten more attention, but it's Fonda's grace and thoughtfulness in *Easy Rider* that made his leather jacket acceptable, even admirable, clothing.

It's important to point out two things about leather and denim. There is an awesome variety of each available these days. Surely too much. You can buy jeans that have been treated to look old and worn or others that are untouched. They come in many colors and shapes. So take the time, and spend the money (these new jeans aren't cheap—though you'll live in them and get your money's worth easily), to get a pair or two that fit you well. There's just no excuse for walking around in ill-fitting jeans these days.

66 Though street style has become much more influenced by hip-hop culture in recent years, it still works on the same vocabulary of leather and denim. 99

And with leather jackets, stick to the tried and true styles. They've been developed over so many years that you can't really improve on them. Racer-style motorcycle jackets (the ones without a collar to fit easily under a helmet) have been making a big comeback lately. Go out and get one and make Peter Fonda proud.

Denim Cowboys: Richard Gere makes the all-denim look seem sexy, above. John Travolta, in Urban Cowboy, left, made us think of black jeans as dressy clothes for a night on the town.

Un-Easy Rider: It's hard to look as nonchalantly hip as Peter Fonda did in Easy Rider, following page. In fact, Fonda never looked that flat-out hip again. If you want to give it a try, make sure you get a racer jacket like this one.

Jeans, Jeans, Everywhere: The biggest fashion trend in years hasn't passed men by. It's all about jeans now. Faded jeans, torn jeans, dirty jeans, dark jeans. Every store has more than you could ever choose from. So think about your jeans the way you would a suit, find two or three styles that suit your personality and maybe a pair for when you're in a particular mood.

"Jeans now come in many colors and shapes. Take the time and spend the money to get a pair or two that fit you well. There's just no excuse for walking around in ill-fitting jeans these days."

Denim, It's Good For You! Steve McQueen does the Western look, left. You can get it too with a wearable denim jacket. Here's a fashion item that never goes out of style, so make sure you get a good one and keep it forever.

TOUGH GUYS DON'T DANCE:

JEANS AND LEATHER AREN'T FOR EVERYONE. AT SOME POINT IN YOUR LIFE YOU'RE GOING TO HAVE TO MAKE A FASHION JUDGMENT CALL: ARE YOU TOUGH OR NOT? THERE'S NOTHING WRONG WITH BEING SENSITIVE; AND TOUGH GUYS ARE OFTEN VASTLY OVERRATED. BUT THE WORST THING YOU CAN BE IN THIS WORLD IS AN EFFETE GUY DRESSED LIKE A FARMHAND.

THE DENIM LEISURE SUIT:

YES, THERE ARE SEVERAL PICTURES HERE OF GUYS WEARING HEAD-TO-TOE DENIM. BUT, IN GENERAL, YOU SHOULD AVOID THE DENIM LEISURE SUIT LOOK AT ALL COSTS. MAKING SURE THAT ALL YOUR JEANS, JEAN JACKETS AND DENIM SHIRTS ARE OF DIFFERENT COLORS WILL GO A LONG WAY TO KEEPING THE SEVENTIES AT BAY.

LEATHER LOVER:

ADMIT IT. YOU WANT A PAIR OF LEATHER PANTS. THERE IS NOTHING WRONG WITH THAT. BUT IT'S ALWAYS BETTER TO OWN A MOTORCYCLE IF YOU'RE GOING TO GO OUT AND GET A PAIR. HOWEVER, IF YOU'RE REALLY DETERMINED, DON'T LET THAT STOP YOU. THE WORLD NEEDS MORE MEN WHO AREN'T AFRAID OF BEING CALLED GAY.

Accessories are Murder

When something goes out of fashion for a very long time—like the boutonniere or spats or the walking stick—it begins to take on an aura of eccentricity, and wearing it becomes a sartorial joke. Just think about what kind of guts it would take to walk into a party sporting a top hat in all seriousness.

What Separates Us from the Apes: It's a man's ability to accessorize that clearly distinguishes him from the garden-variety slob roaming the streets. Take Peter Sellers (previous page): His glasses and matching tie and pocket square give him a distinctive appearance. Kirk Douglas is clearly no match for him.
Just look what a hat, tie and braces do for Sylvester Stallone.

Obviously some items deserve to fall into neglect. Either modern materials better serve the original purpose, or changing times have eliminated the need. Who would want to wear those silly little garters to hold up your socks? (But, believe it or not, there are men who go out of their way to find the original hose without elastic.)

Many men's accessories have suffered this near obsolescence. Suspenders, hats and all sorts of silks are things you just don't see on men anymore. Which is part of what makes men's clothes much less appealing these days. A good suit is like the foundation of a building: solid but just the start. The right combination of shoes, suspenders, tie and pocket square can take a suit and completely re-invent it.

Through the Looking Glass: Burt Lancaster, Woody Allen and David Hemmings demonstrate the importance of glasses in making or altering a man's image. While Woody Allen might not get recognized without his glasses, Hemmings takes on an effete air and Lancaster's famous athleticism is softened by his unexpectedly bookish sunglasses.

66 The right com-bination of shoes, suspenders, tie and pocket square can take a suit and completely re-invent it. 99

SHOES

I've met many men who try to conserve their budgets by attempting to get by on one or two pairs of shoes. And though it can be done, rotating each pair so the other gets a day of rest and keeping them well shined, you have to wonder if that sort of guy has his heart in the right place. Would he appreciate the puckish humor of a pair of brown suede shoes? How could he pass up the opportunity to own some casual yet stylish pairs, which can be used to dress a suit down, or some pairs flashy enough to transform the same suit for a night out?

Good shoes aren't easy on the budget, that's certainly true. After a suit, they're one of the bigger expenditures. But cared for properly, shoes will really last. And if you pace yourself over time, you might be able to put together a serious arsenal. Obviously you need a pair of shiny black shoes in calfskin with a cap toe or just a plain vamp to dress up your blue and grey suits for serious meetings and somber events. Then you will need a lighter brown pair to make those same clothes feel a little more adventurous and Italian. The Italians were, after all, the ones who made it okay to wear brown shoes with blue suits (though it was the English who paired lush grey flannel with brown suede, a combination that defines sublime). After those basics, you're sure to need some shoes with brogueing, a distinctive pattern of perforation that decorates men's shoes. At this point, you'll want to declare your allegiance to either brown or black, as most men have a preference. Nonetheless, you should force yourself to buy the opposite color once every four or five pairs just to be sure.

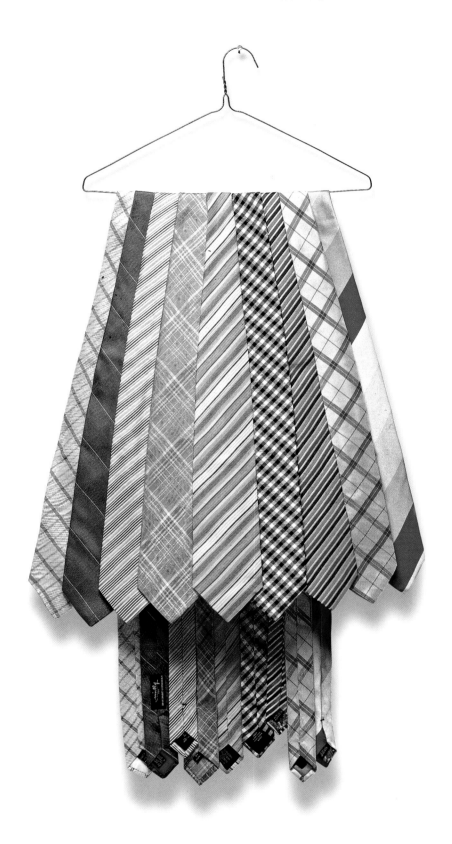

Previous pages: He's got the Power: Fred Astaire illustrates the transformative powers of accessories.
Name Above the Title: Douglas Fairbanks, Jr. makes his tie the centerpiece of his outfit. There's no reason you can't either. But try to ensure the tie plays some sort of role in relation to the rest of your clothes by either complementing them or contrasting with them. All too often men choose a tie as if it were the only item of clothing they were wearing that day.

Tie Me Up, Tie Me Down: Choosing a tie is only half the battle of getting dressed. You've still got to knot the damn thing into something presentable. It doesn't matter so much which type of knot you choose (some mathematicians figured out that there are some eighty-oddpossible knots) as much as that you tie the knot neatly and make sure it comes out with a good dimple. A dimple? Yes, a dimple. Douglas Fairbanks, Jr. knows that the secret to a sophisticated look is a dimple just below the knot of your tie.

TIES

Ties are a man's arsenal. From its dominant position on your chest, a tie sets the tone of who you are and what you want to convey. You should think about acquiring ties the way a warrior stockpiles weapons. Some ties, like stripes, polka dots and other large patterns, are workhorses that you'll wear often because they bring harmony to colors in your suits and combine well with smaller patterns. More intricate patterns, such as paisleys and other complicated prints, will demand a feature role. But the mistake too many men make is thinking that their tie exists in a world all its own. They wear a tie not as part of a whole but like a flag flying out in front of them. A tie can be anything from a loud counterpoint to a gentle reworking of the themes in the rest of your clothes.

HOW TO CHOOSE A TIE KNOT:

THE FOUR-IN-HAND IS REALLY THE WORKHORSE OF TIE KNOTS. IT LOOKS GOOD WITHOUT BEING TOO PRISSY OR STUDIED AND THE LOPSIDEDNESS ACTUALLY GIVES IT A CERTAIN DEVIL-MAY-CARE FLAIR. AND WHEN YOU THINK ABOUT IT, THAT'S REALLY THE HEIGHT OF FASHION. BUT IF YOU'RE GOING FOR A MORE POLISHED LOOK, AND THAT'S CERTAINLY YOUR PREROGA-TIVE, YOU'LL USE SOME VERSION OF THE WINDSOR KNOT, EITHER THE HALF-WINDSOR OR THE FULL WINDSOR. THIS KNOT GIVES A MORE STRAIGHTFORWARD TRIANGULAR APPEARANCE, WITH THE FULL WINDSOR LOOKING LIKE AN EQUILATERAL TRIANGLE POINTING DOWN FROM BENEATH YOUR CHIN (WHICH IS A GOOD REASON TO AVOID THE HALF-WINDSOR BECAUSE THAT KNOT WINDS UP BEING NEITHER FISH NOR FOWL.) THE WINDSOR KNOT HELPS TO FILL IN THE SPREADS ON THE POPULAR SPREAD-COLLAR SHIRTS, BUT MANY MEN WHO CHOOSE THIS KNOT EMPLOY IT WITH A NUMBING REGULARITY. IT'S THE TIE-KNOT EQUIVALENT OF SLICKED-BACK HAIR. AND THOSE WHO SELECT IT BECAUSE THEY THINK THEY'RE FOLLOWING THE LEAD OF THE DUKE OF WINDSOR ARE BEING DOUBLY DECEIVED. THE DUKE WAS FOND OF A THICK KNOT TO FILL IN HIS SPREAD COLLARS. BUT HE SIMPLY HAD HIS TAILORS MAKE HIM SPECIAL FAT TIES. THE WINDSOR KNOT WAS A MASS-MARKET INVENTION FOR GUYS WHO WANTED THE WINDSOR LOOK, BUT DIDN'T HAVE ACCESS TO FLEET OF PERSONAL TIE MAKERS. THE TRUE SPIRITUAL DESCENDANT OF THE DUKE'S THICK KNOT IS THE NEAPOLITAN LOOK YOU GET FROM BORELLI OR KITON. USING WIDE TIES, THE ITALIANS CREATE CHUNKY KNOTS OUT OF SIMPLE FOUR-IN-HAND KNOTS. IT'S A DISTINCTIVE KNOT, BUT NOT FOR EVERYONE. GIVE IT A TRY THOUGH, AND YOU'LL GIVE YOUR WARDROBE A WHOLE NEW LEASE ON LIFE.

Penn Pal: A hat doesn't have to be fancy to be rakish or cool. Sean Penn gave surfer chic a shot in the arm in Fast Times at Ridgemont High, left. Andy Garcia gets a lot of mileage out of a Panama hat, below.

HATS

The most famous hat in the movies has to be Indiana Jones's fedora. The sturdy felt hat paired with a leather jacket gave Harrison Ford just the right combination of dashing presence and professorial rectitude. But these days wearing a hat is more of a statement. Men used to need to wear hats to keep warm and ward off the rain. Now, in our temperature-controlled enviroment, hats are really just style items. Although you can get through the milder seasons without a coat by wearing a nice hat with your suits, that's not a common look. Instead, find a hat that you connect with on an emotional level. The more you identify with your hat, the more likely you are to wear it.

HATS OFF:

IF YOU'RE LIKE MOST MEN, YOU OWN ONE HAT. YOU MIGHT HAVE BOUGHT IT ON VACATION, OR IT'S YOUR FAVORITE BASEBALL CAP CREASED, FOLDED AND STAINED. WHATEVER THAT HAT IS, I GUARANTEE YOU NEED ANOTHER ONE. EVERYONE WONDERS WHAT KILLED HAT WEARING. SOME PEOPLE LIKE TO REPEAT THAT OLD SAW ABOUT JOHN F. KENNEDY, BUT I THINK CARS KILLED HATS MORE THAN ANYTHING ELSE. TRY GETTING INTO A CAR WITH A DECENT HAT ON AND YOU'LL QUICKLY GROW TIRED OF TAKING IT OFF AND LOOKING FOR A PLACE TO PUT IT.

WITH THAT IN MIND, MAKE SURE YOU HAVE A COUPLE OF DIFFERENT HATS FOR A VARIETY OF OCCASIONS. DON'T GET A FEDORA UNLESS YOU CAN CARRY ONE OFF. BUT THAT DOESN'T MEAN THERE ISN'T A GREAT VARIETY OF CLASSIC MEN'S HATS TO CHOOSE FROM. MOST HAVE A VARIETY OF NAMES, SO LET'S NOT BORE YOU WITH THEM HERE. BUT THINK ABOUT GETTING BEYOND THAT BASEBALL CAP AND TRYING SOMETHING DIFFERENT. JUST REMEMBER TO WEAR THE HAT; DON'T LET THE HAT WEAR YOU.

Cover Art: Humphrey Bogart is dressed for riding but he's wearing a stylish street hat. Paul Newman brings out the best in his argyle sweater with English cap. Nat Cole adds a little country-club soul to a practice session. Jean-Paul Belmondo gives the hat a just-out-of-bed slant.

LINKS-A-LOT:

LET'S JUST START BY SAYING THAT CUFFLINKS ARE LIKE CRACK: ONCE YOU START, YOU'RE STUCK WITH THE HABIT. AND THEY DON'T COME CHEAP. SURE, CUFFLINKS ARE THE HEIGHT OF STYLE, BUT THEY ARE A RICH MAN'S PASSION. NOT ONLY DO YOU NEED FRENCH CUFFS ON YOUR SHIRTS TO WEAR THEM, THE BEST ARE MADE FROM PRECIOUS METALS, OR WITH PRECIOUS STONES AND OFTEN EMPLOY ARTISAN TECHNIQUES SUCH AS ENAMELING THAT MAKE FOR BEAUTIFUL OBJECTS BUT REQUIRE A MAN TO HAVE NUMER-OUS PAIRS. YOU DON'T WANT TO BE SEEN WEARING THE SAME CUFFLINKS DAY-IN AND DAY-OUT. IF YOU DO DECIDE TO TAKE THE PLUNGE, START WITH A METAL PAIR THAT WILL GO WITH ANY COLOR SHIRT. THEN BUILD OUT UNTIL YOU'VE GOT A DECENT COLLECTION THAT'S COLOR COORDINATED WITH YOUR SHIRTS. IF YOU'VE STILL GOT SOME MONEY LEFT OVER, CONGRATULATIONS, YOU'RE A RICH MAN.

He Did it His Way: Frank Sinatra flexes his smoking muscle to show off some serious square links.

SUSPENDERS

The British call suspenders braces mostly because there is already a garment called suspenders: Americans call that garment a garter belt. Braces aren't quite as sexy on men as garter belts are on women but they have the same antique appeal. Few men wear braces today because they require such a commitment. That commitment is more than simply having some buttons sewn in your pants: To wear braces well, your pants need to be cut looser in the waist so they drape well. Once you've made the leap though, there are many rewards. Your suits will be more comfortable, and the braces themselves offer another opportunity to mix color and pattern into your wardrobe. Working off the pattern and color of your tie, your braces can be anything from a colorful counterpoint (bright red-and-yellow plaid braces under a blue suit, blue shirt and tie), to a subtle underlining of the colors in the rest of your outfit.

Braced Up: Gary Cooper comes through again, right, with a perfect pair of suspenders holding up some very high-waisted pants.

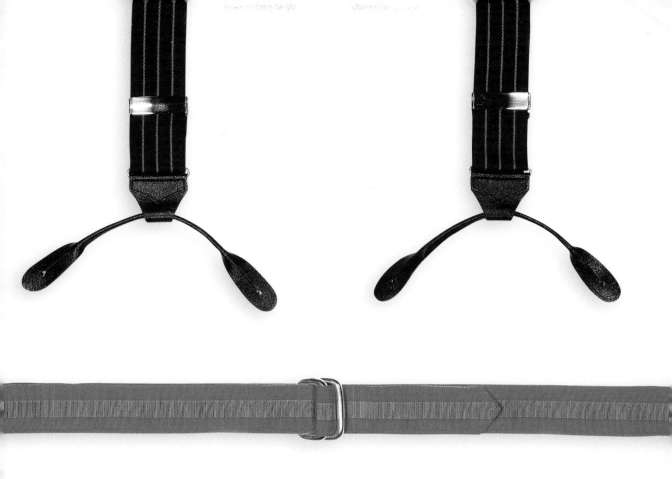

BRACE YOURSELF:

SUSPENDERS ARE THERE TO LET YOUR PANTS HANG FROM THE SHOULDERS INSTEAD OF BEING CINCHED AT THE WAIST. THIS GIVES YOUR PANTS A DRAPED LINE INSTEAD OF HAVING THEM CLING TO YOUR HIPS AND BACKSIDE. IT'S A DIFFERENT LOOK THAN MOST MEN ARE ACCUSTOMED TO THESE DAYS. FIRST, YOUR PANTS SHOULD BE CUT HIGHER, WITH A LONGER RISE, SO THE FABRIC WILL DRAPE FROM YOUR NATURAL WAIST. SECOND, YOUR PANTS WILL HANG LOOSELY AROUND YOUR MIDDLE, WHICH IS MORE COMFORTABLE EVEN IF AT FIRST YOU FEEL LIKE YOU'RE WEARING A BARREL INSTEAD OF A SUIT. FINALLY, SUSPENDERS ARE ONE MORE WAY TO GET COLOR AND TEXTURE INTO YOUR WARDROBE. SINCE SUSPENDERS ARE AN ACQUIRED TASTE, STORES TEND TO STOCK ONLY THE LARGE SIZE UNDER THE THEORY THAT THEY CAN BE ADJUSTED TO FIT ANYONE. THIS LEAVES MANY SMALLER MEN WITH THE CLASPS RIDING HIGH ON THEIR CLAVICLES. ONCE YOU'VE MADE THE COMMITMENT, HOWEVER, YOU MIGHT WONDER WHY YOU EVER BOTHERED WEARING A BELT. THAT IS, UNTIL THE HUMIDITY GOES OFF THE CHARTS AND YOU'RE WISHING YOU STILL HAD BELT LOOPS ON YOUR PANTS.

SCARVES AND HANDKERCHIEFS

Rather than facing out-and-out extinction—the scarf probably has the worst possible reputation of all accessories due its ready association with effeminate queens and pompous millionaires—the scarf survives like some prehistoric fish, out of sight but waiting for its opportunity to thrive again.

Why has the time-honored habit of covering one's neck fallen so far out of favor? Perhaps it's because the scarf originally was meant as a substitute for the necktie, which is now itself fairly moribund. Maybe that's why the only men who have been seen in neckerchiefs in the last twenty years of the movies have been absurd characters whose choice of a poncy scarf immediately signaled their utter irrelevance to a story.

But the scarf is a robust addition to any wardrobe and more useful in our current casual times than ever before. If the central tenet of being well dressed is to keep one's clothes restrained and coordinated (think of the ideal outfits that

have survived so many eras: grey flannels and blue blazers, khakis and white shirts), then the perfect final touch is a piece of silk (or cotton) around the neck. Al Pacino wears one in The *Godfather III*, and once you've seen it, it will dispel any thoughts you ever had that a scarf signals weakness. Dressed in black, his silver neckerchief—no bigger than a bandana and tied around his neck in a neat square-knot—marks Michael Corleone as a sophisticated European with a menacing character. Without the neatly knotted cloth, Pacino would just look like any other middling man dressed in black. With it, he becomes a warrior, the prince of his family and worldly character. That's a lot of work for a little scarf.

Part of the problem is simply finding a scarf that will work. Women's prints are too complicated, and it's hard to find a large masculine print on a decent-sized scarf anymore. That doesn't mean they don't exist, you just have to look for them. While you're searching, try a solid-colored scarf or just take a thin silk scarf made for winter and knot it loosely under a shirt. You won't notice the extra fabric anymore than you would a T-shirt.

Other options are to take a silk pocket square, fold it like a bandana (make a triangle, then roll from the point down to the base—that will give you a smooth surface), and then tie it with a square knot at the base of your neck. The color and silk will dress up a polo shirt and jeans. And, as long as you choose a simple color like navy blue, the scarf will give you just that accent of color that shows you put some thought into getting dressed that morning.

Scarf it down! Clark Gable keeps it warm aboard ship; Edward Fox exemplifies the dashing look a scarf can give a man in The Day of the Jackal; Robert Redford's Gatsby looks for the green light; and David Hemmings adds a bit of sass to his English country clothes.

From there you can work your way up to larger scarves in more complicated knots. The standard tie knot, a four-in-hand, will help the scarf hang straight down your shirt. But with a larger scarf, you might want to tie the first part of a bow and then slip one end over the top. That will give you the best part of the Ascot look without having to buy one of those cheesy pre-sewn Ascots, which are strictly amateur. Wearing one of those is like using a clip-on bowtie.

Stripes and Patterns

Any guy can learn to dress well in a decent blue suit, a white shirt and a subtle tie. Your look will be elegantly understated and you'll give off the air of man who knows who he is and what he wants. Then, you can take that basic idea and add a little bit of color, say a nice cornflower blue shirt and a yellow tie for contrast. Once you've mastered colors, there's only one mountain left to climb: Stripes and patterns. Stripes come into a man's wardrobe first, and a bold tie or even a T-shirt work well as striking visual accents.

Stripers: From subtle accents to bold statements, stripes are the first weapon in a man's wardrobe. That's something Humphrey Bogart amply demonstrates, previous page, with a dark wardrobe heightened by pin stripes on his suit and tie. You have to ask yourself which is more menacing, the clothes or the gun? Tyrone Power, right, pairs a striking striped tie with attention-grabbing two-toned shoes for maximum impact.

You're very likely to want to include a number of striped shirts in your wardrobe. You'll think you're quite smart wearing a navy blue suit with a light blue Bengal striped shirt. If you're going casual to the office you could leave off the tie and still look like a heavyweight. Then there's the clubby checked dress shirt in the English style, where two striking colors are set against each other in a big check. The shirts are beautiful, but one must be careful when choosing a tie. The safe route is a solid colored tie in the same shade as the overplaid. But you can also use larger scale patterns, such as polka dots, as long as the ground of the tie uses a color that matches the shirts.

When you want to get into the ring with other serious clothescocks, however, you'll have to start working with the complexities of patterns and stripes in your suits as well as your shirts and ties. Eventually, you'll start combining them in ways that may appear to vibrate out of control. To get it right, you'll even need to go over the edge a few times—just to teach yourself a lesson.

> **" Mixing patterns is the big leagues of dressing. It shows that you pick your own clothes and can do it with authority, humor and adventurousness. Aren't those traits you want to present to the world? "**

As with everything in life, with menswear, you should start with the basics and work your way up in complexity. For example, the Glen plaid suit is a classic, a very English fabric (it's often called a Prince of Wales check because it was made popular by Edward when he was Prince in the nineteen-twenties and thirties). Unfortunately, you don't see very much of it these days. Its scarcity is surely a product of the last two decades of Italian chic. If you want to see it in action over a fifty-year period, just look at Cary Grant in *His Girl Friday*, then rent *48 Hours* and see how Eddie Murphy puts an eighties spin on the suit, wearing it with a collar pin. You can also check out *Scent of a Woman* where Al Pacino wears one and pairs it with a burgundy tie. In the mirror, the burgundy tie might look a little off, but in normal conversational range the two colors will complement each other nicely.

Pattern Pride: John Huston, above, gets a kick out of his matching plaid hat and jacket.

If Glen plaid isn't your style, there are a number of other classic patterns that are well worth exploring. The biggest problem with men's suits today is that the muted patterns take the fun out of dressing. There's just no point to washed-out pin stripes or muted overplaids. It's as if men want a little variety, but are afraid to be seen in a bold suit. If you're ready to dress with some authority, look for patterns that ask to be noticed. Pin stripes, which come in a huge variety of colors, should be highly contrasted and legible. Humphrey Bogart regularly wears a serious pin stripe suit. Jimmy Stewart wears one very well in *The Philadelphia Story* and no one ever described him as a loud dresser.

Here's Looking at You, Kid: Bogart wears a classic striped shirt that gives him a casual yet commanding presence. The same shirt can be seen on Frank Sinatra, James Dean and other stars through the years.

A windowpane plaid provides a nice alternative to pin stripes. You get the same contrast, usually a blue or grey suit, with a brighter box plaid stitched into it. Nick Nolte wears a superb example in *I Love Trouble*, a movie forgettable for everything but Nolte's clothes. Big guys are better suited to patterns because the busyness doesn't overwhelm them. If you're smaller in stature, take care in choosing a suit with a finer gauge to the plaid—or stick with pin stripes, which definitely give you the added impression of verticality.

However, stripes and plaids aren't the only patterns. William Powell, one of the legendary male movie stars whose clothes were always his calling card, wears patterns, such as a houndstooth, with striped ties to give himself a casual yet elegant air. The combination, pulled off so innocently, is a constant reminder that he has mastered the art of dressing.

Go Ahead: You don't have to be as tough as Dirty Harry to take the risk and combine patterns, although you might want to avoid Harry's polyblends. Not even a .44 will make those look impressive.

Stars and Bars: In Casino, left, Robert DeNiro wears a striking windowpane suit. His outfit gets its kick from the vivid shirt-and-tie combination. You can do the same, above, by pairing a bright tie with a bright shirt or vest. An almost ordinary seersucker suit suddenly becomes a dandyish outfit.

SUITS ME FINE:

IT'S IMPORTANT TO REMEMBER WHEN YOU'RE ABOUT TO PLUNK DOWN SOME SERIOUS COIN ON A POWERFULLY PATTERNED SUIT THAT PEOPLE WILL RECALL IT EVERY TIME YOU WEAR IT. MAKE SURE THAT YOU HAVE A DECENT ARRAY OF BLUE, BROWN AND GREY SUITS THAT PAIR EASILY WITH PATTERNED SHIRTS AND TIES BEFORE COMMITTING TO THAT ENERGETIC PIN STRIPE OR LAVENDER WINDOWPANE. SUCH STRIKING SUITS ARE GETTING MORE POPULAR THESE DAYS, BUT MOST MEN WHO OWN THEM KNOW THAT THEY WILL HAVE TO WEAR LAVENDER SHIRTS WITH THAT WINDOWPANE. IF YOU THINK YOU'RE GOING TO GET AWAY WITH IT AS AN EVERYDAY WARDROBE ITEM, GUESS AGAIN.

GET YOUR SEA LEGS:

MATING PATTERNS OR PAIRING PATTERNS AND STRIPES IS AN ART, NOT A SCIENCE. SOME MEN HAVE A NATURAL ABILITY TO COMBINE WHAT MIGHT OTHERWISE SEEM TO BE CLASHING PAT-TERNS. BUT IF YOU DON'T HAVE THE KNACK, THAT DOESN'T MEAN YOU CAN'T TRAIN YOURSELF TO SPOT A GOOD COMBINATION. START WITH A CONSTANT COLOR, SAY, BLUE; NEXT TRY TO PUT A SIMPLE BLUE-AND-WHITE STRIPED SHIRT TOGETHER WITH A BLUE-AND-WHITE POLKA-DOT TIE. GET THAT TO WORK A COUPLE OF TIMES AND YOU'RE READY TO EXPERIMENT WITH A BLUE-AND-WHITE STRIPED TIE AND BLUE-AND-WHITE CHECKED SHIRT. THEN START PLAYING WITH THE SCALE OF CHECK, STRIPE AND DOT.

THE AMAZING TECHNICOLOR DREAMCOAT:

ONCE YOU'VE GOT SCALE DOWN, YOU'LL BE READY TO PLAY WITH COLOR. THE FIRST THING TO REMEMBER WHEN MIXING PATTERNS IS THAT YOU NEED TO KEEP WITHIN A COLOR THEME. THAT MEANS HOLDING ONE COLOR CONSTANT ACROSS ALL YOUR PATTERNS (WHITE DOESN'T COUNT AS A COLOR IF YOU LET THE OTHER COLORS CLASH). GOT THAT? FOR EXTRA CREDIT YOU CAN USE VARIATIONS ON A COLOR AS YOUR THEME, SUCH AS COMBINING BURGUNDY, RED, BROWN AND RUST.

Bold Strokes: Choose your accessories well. A strong argyle sweater with a good mix of colors, right, will liven up a number of suits and jackets. These accent pieces are what make a wardrobe work without a heavy investment.

Criss-Cross: Same-color patterns mix best when you pay attention to scale. A bright, striped tie, following page, works with this checked shirt because they are in perfect balance. Remember, it's not as easy as some people make it look.

DON'T WORRY ABOUT GETTING YOUR PAT-
TERNS OR COLORS WRONG. YOU'LL HAVE
TO TAKE RISKS WHEN YOU DECIDE TO
DRESS THIS WAY. THAT'S THE FUN OF IT. IF
YOU DIDN'T PUSH THINGS TOO FAR ON
OCCASION THEN YOU MIGHT AS WELL HAVE
SOMEONE CHOOSE YOUR CLOTHES FOR
YOU, OR OPT FOR A BLACK MAO SUIT.
MAGNIFICENT FAILURES ARE WHAT
DANDYISM IS ALL ABOUT. BESIDES, THE
ONLY TIME YOU REALLY LEARN IN DRESS-
ING IS WHEN YOU MAKEMISTAKES. YOU'LL
NEVER EVEN KNOW IF IT'S A MISTAKE
UNLESS YOU TAKE THE RISK AND WALK
OUT THE DOOR WITH THAT COMBINATION
YOU'RE NOT ENTIRELY SURE OF.

Power Surge: Tyrone Power gets it going on all
levels with a Glen plaid suit, plaid tie and argyle
socks, previous page. Notice the white shirt
keeps the whole ensemble from tilting over into
clashing. The ensemble opposite him is an
example of how related colors can pull different
patterns together.

Oooh, Breathless: Jean-Paul Belmondo, left, is
still cool decades after Breathless was shot. You
don't have to be Jean Seberg to appreciate his
nonchalant style or admire his pencil stripe shirt
and shepherd's check tie.

Bring on the White

If you look back at the way men used to dress, it's hard not to be struck by the fact that no one wears white anymore. In the nineteenth century, white was the most fashionable summer color for men. Before air conditioning, summer clothes were prized more for their open weaves and ability to reflect the heat than for any great variety of hue.

Memorial Day: Humphrey Bogart relaxes around the house in this publicity shot, previous page. Johnny Depp goes glam in the seventies period-piece Blow. Both actors changed their familiar screen personas simply by donning white suits.

So, for comfort, men were content to confine their wardrobe to a limited palette: a range of light colors that ran roughly from pig-white seersuckers to nearly tan linen. Daniel Day-Lewis exemplifies this in *The Age of Innocence*; Dirk Bogarde gives it a Central European spin in *Death in Venice*; and Gary Cooper shows how chic it was during the 1930s in *Now and Forever*, a movie set on the French Riviera.

We have, I'm sure, many valid reasons for the loss of white: fabrics are now lighter and cooler, and our environment is increasingly air-conditioned from home to the car to work and back again. Moreover, few men are comfortable wearing clothes that make them feel so vulnerable. Stains and smudges, it would seem, are only the beginning of their fears.

Many men seem to think white is too feminine for them. So how to explain why Debra Winger races to catch the ferry in *An Officer and Gentleman*? Nor does this bias accommodate for how fierce Louis Gossett, Jr. looks in a similar white uniform. Perhaps guys who worry about looking tough enough should see Orson Welles play a hard-bitten sailor in *The Lady from Shanghai*. The loose-fitting white tunic he wears over white pants through much of the movie does nothing to dispel the sexual tension hanging over him and Rita Hayworth. In fact, the sailor's whites add something to the movie's entire tone of dissolution.

White is sometimes used to transform our presentations of well-established characters. Humphrey Bogart has one of the toughest screen personas ever created, but his white dinner jacket in *Casablanca* (or the tropical whites he wears as an escaped convict with a heart of gold in *We're No Angels*) softens our stance toward him. Suddenly it's not so hard to imagine him as a casino owner with a heart of gold.

White may bring to mind purity and innocence when women wear it, but on men it has been more often associated with dandyism. Johnny Depp's drug dealer in *Blow* isn't far from John Lennon when he and Yoko were first married. Robert Redford played up Jay Gatsby's dandyism, as well as his tragic nature, with his immaculate white outfits.

Gatsby's Great: Robert Redford, below, in The Great Gatsby wears a white suit without going all-white.

Good Humor Man: Gary Cooper looks refreshing and immaculate at the races in his double-breasted white suit, pale tie and white pocket square.

> **66 The secret to wearing white is to make sure that what you're wearing mixes various textures and hues. 99**

Such tragic overtones may not be what you bargained for, but they're no reason to abjure white. If you do wear white take this one precaution: you'll want to avoid the studied attempt at gangster cool that you see in P. Diddy's spic-and-span outfits. Instead, think about James Dean swanning through *East of Eden* in a near-perfect assemblage of cream-colored flannel pants and a white shirt under a parchment-white sweater vest. The true power of white is best seen in the subtle overlapping of white and whitelike tones. In fact, the secret to wearing white is to make sure that what you're wearing mixes various textures and hues.

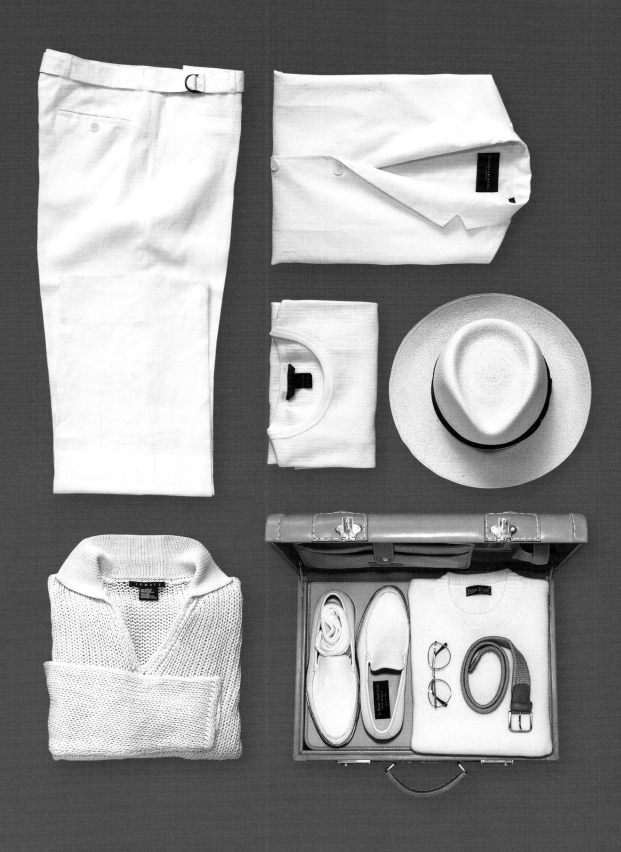

Tone, Tone, Tone: Douglas Fairbanks, Jr. shows off the ideal layering of white tones, left. You can do the same by making sure your white items span the range from bone and cream to eggshell and laundry white. Don't forget to have a selection of textures easily at hand, like this loose-knit sweater or a Panama hat.

Hang Time: The perfect white shirt will give even the most casual occasion an air of formality. But to have the perfect white shirt for all occasions means having several different kinds on hand.

An Easy Lay: Layering your whites and off-whites gives an all-white outfit texture and variety. It also avoids the studied perfection of matched hues.

White's All Right: Harry Belafonte relaxes in the film Island in the Sun.

Black
Attack

When you get dressed you want to make an impression—even if it's not a good one. I'm not saying that you want to cause a problem, but plenty of guys want to make it clear they don't entirely fit in. They're guys who could go either way—they could do the right thing or they could do wrong—and, indeed, sometimes both. So it's no wonder that most guys who feel like outsiders, either socially or emotionally, start dressing in black at some point.

The all-black outfit—either the head-to-toe blackout or just the black suit and tie over a white shirt—is a staple of the movies and it's shame we don't see it more on the streets. Just think of that indelible scene in *Reservoir Dogs* where the whole crew of thieves, dressed identically in black suits, white shirts and black ties, walk through the diner parking lot to their cars. The rhythm of black suits repeated across so many obviously dangerous men only increases the dread we all feel when watching it. You can see the same thing in Quentin Tarantino's other gangster classic *Pulp Fiction,* where John Travolta's diffidence radiates from his black suit.

You Can't Refuse: Al Pacino looks suitably ruthless in The Godfather, previous page. Ethan Hawke, above, wears black for an ultra-modern futuristic look in Gattaca.

The message is reversed in *Men in Black* where Tommy Lee Jones and Will Smith play two outwardly innocuous, even aggressively banal, men. But, as the movie shows, their extraordinary lives are hidden from view and effaced by their special powers. In both types of movies, it's the antique conformity of the clothes that suggests something about the truly nonconforming personalities that lie underneath. The bonus in *Men in Black* is that their characters are decent men instead of sociopathic hard cases.

Black doesn't always make a statement about the characters themselves, but often about the circumstances around them. Every heist picture (like *Ocean's Eleven,* the original and the remake) or commando flick (like *The Guns of Navarone*) has several scenes where the actors slink around in black sweaters and slick-looking black cargo pants. The clothes, as cool as they

Reservoir of Power: Quentin Tarantino, right, mixed retro chic with the workman's uniform to create this powerful visual metaphor in Reservoir Dogs. His anonymous gangsters know little about each other and get caught in a job that goes unbelievably bad. Their clothes capture the alienating and dehumanizing aspects of their lives. They look pretty damn cool, too.

Black Out: The best black outfits match perfectly in hue, previous page. Subtle differences in materials like silk and cotton become rich details when the color is in sync. But, as Clint Eastwood demonstrates, you don't have to go for the full black-out to achieve presence.

Shanghai Surprise: Orson Welles in the bewildering final scene of The Lady from Shanghai, above. His black suit and tie convey the movie's final triumph of cynicism over romantic love. Keanu Reeves, right, and the rest of the cast in The Matrix turn the cliches about men in black upside down.

may look, have no more importance than a pair of coveralls. However, in one of the most stylish men's movies ever made, *Shaft*, the shift into all-black commando gear has social and political overtones that go far beyond the utilitarian need to avoid being seen.

Richard Roundtree pioneers the seventies style of wearing suits in classic woolen patterns over solid colored turtlenecks. The look was the answer to the assault in the late sixties on the suit-and-tie orthodoxy. But no matter how elegant Shaft looks in his street clothes, the most memorable ensemble in the movie is Roundtree's action gear of black leather pants, a black turtleneck sweater and a long coal-black leather trenchcoat. Shaft appears dressed that way in only one climactic scene, which is, essentially, a commando raid itself.

Penn State: Sean Penn in *State of Grace* epitomizes the lone lawman in search of justice.

No one watching the movie in 1971 could miss director Gordon Parks's reference to the Black Panthers, who paraded through the sixties dressed all in black and carrying shotguns. Similarly, Roundtree's Shaft donned black to take the law into his own hands. The point of the movie was that Shaft was an outsider to both the black world and the white establishment. He was a loner at a time when that actually meant something—and his willingness to take the law into his own hands was truly a political act (that, after all, was the message of the Black Panthers).

Not every black shirt is necessarily a political act. By the year 2000, Samuel L. Jackson played Shaft in an exceedingly cool all-black Armani suit, but by then the effect was curtailed. The social context of *Shaft* in 2000 was more about simply looking cool. Jackson did look cool, but he couldn't be Shaft—he was just "one bad mother," as the song says.

This is the usual message black sends: In the movies, the character in black is a menace (one of the best examples of this is Gary Oldman playing a psychopathic Irish gangster on New York's west side in *State of Grace*) or a mess (James Spader mopes through *Sex, Lies and Videotape* in a coal-black shirt that matches his unchanging mood.)

Back in Black: High polish brings out the best in black.

Black to the Future: The tiniest details come to life in black clothing.
Notice the added panache of a pebbled sole or an extra barrel-cuff button or some special stitching.

Dean's List: James Dean cools his heels off the set in a simple black polo shirt.

But it's in the Westerns that black has its richest history. The classic protagonist of the Western is the self-reliant man who brings his own moral code to a lawless world. It's someone like Henry Fonda playing Wyatt Earp in *My Darling Clementine*. Fonda's brooding lawman is the forefather of every laconic drifter from Clint Eastwood's *Man with No Name* to Mel Gibson's *Mad Max*. It's no accident that Fonda strides through the movie in head-to-toe black save for a tiny swath of white shirt supporting his black string tie. To see him slouching on the porch of the Tombstone jail with his foot propped up against the post is to witness the true birth of masculine cool.

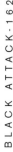

"It's no wonder that most guys who feel like outsiders, either socially or emotionally, start dressing in black at some point."

Talkin' 'bout Shaft: Richard Roundtree gets more mileage out of wearing black in one scene of the original Shaft than Samuel L. Jackson did in wearing nothing but black in the remake.

Boys in the Band: Early in their career, before they got turned into the loveable moptops, the Beatles had tough-guy demeanor and a black wardrobe reminiscent of Johnny Cash and the rockabilly outlaws they admired.

Photo Credits

4: James Garner © Tom Caffrey; 7: Clark Gable © George Hurrell, courtesy of MPTV; 9: Ben Affleck, courtesy of Photofest; 10: Burt Reynolds © Gene Trindl, courtesy of MPTV; 12: Peter Lawford, courtesy of Everett Collection; 13: Jean-Paul Belmondo in *Breathless*, courtesy of Everett Collection; 13: Sammy Davis Jr., courtesy of Photofest; 15: Warren Beatty in *Bugsy* © Tristar Pictures, courtesy of Photofest; 16: Steve McQueen © William Claxton; 17: Steve McQueen © William Claxton; 18-19: Fred Astaire, courtesy of MPTV; 21: Steve McQueen in *The Thomas Crown Affair*, courtesy of Everett Collection; 22: Ray Liotta, Robert DeNiro, Paul Sorvino, Joe Pesci in *Goodfellas*, courtesy of MPTV; 23: Gary Cooper, courtesy of Everett Collection; 24: Robert Redford in *The Candidate*, courtesy of Photofest; 25: Clark Gable, courtesy of Everett Collection; 26: Michael Douglas in *Wall Street*, courtesy of Photofest; 27: Tom Cruise in *Rain Man*, courtesy of Photofest; 30: Cary Grant in *The Philadelphia Story*, courtesy of Everett Collection; 30: Robert Redford in *The Great Gatsby*, courtesy of Everett Collection; 31: Mick Jagger, courtesy of Everett Collection; 31: Fred Astaire, courtesy of Everett Collection; 32: Gary Cooper, courtesy of Photofest; 34-35: Peter Lawford, Dean Martin, Sammy Davis Jr., Frank Sinatra in *Ocean's Eleven*, courtesy of Everett Collection; 37: Gary Cooper, courtesy of Photofest; 38: Jack Nicholson and Angelica Huston, courtesy of Everett Collection; 39: Frank Sinatra, courtesy of Everett Collection; 40: Steve McQueen in *The Thomas Crown Affair*, courtesy of Everett Collection; 41: Billy Zane in *Titanic*, courtesy of Photofest; 42: James Dean © Corbis; 43: Sean Connery in *Goldfinger*, courtesy of Photofest; 44: Cary Grant, courtesy of MPTV; 48: Nat King Cole, courtesy of MPTV; 51: Marcello Mastroianni in *La Dolce Vita*, courtesy of Everett Collection; 52: Jude Law and Matt Damon in *The Talented Mr. Ripley*, courtesy of Everett Collection; 53: Mickey Rourke in *9 1/2 Weeks*, courtesy of Photofest; 54: Clark Gable, courtesy of Photofest; 56: Michael Douglas in *Streets of San Francisco*, courtesy of MPTV; 60-61: George Clooney and Brad Pitt in *Ocean's Eleven*, courtesy of Photofest; 63: Steve McQueen and Fay Dunaway in *The Thomas Crown Affair*, courtesy of Everett Collection; 64: Cary Grant in *To Catch A Thief*, courtesy of Everett Collection; 66: Kirk Douglas, courtesy of Everett Collection; 67: Paul Michael Glaser and David Soul in *Starsky and Hutch*, courtesy of MPTV; 70: Robert Taylor, courtesy of Everett Collection; 70: Clark Gable © George Hurrell, courtesy of MPTV; 72: Steve McQueen in *The Thomas Crown Affair*, courtesy of MPTV; 74: Brad Pitt in *A River Runs Through It*, courtesy of MPTV; 77: John Travolta in *Grease*, courtesy of MPTV; 80: John Travolta in *Pulp Fiction* © MPTV ; 82: Brad Pitt in *Fight Club*, courtesy of Photofest; 85: Tony Curtis © Leo Choplin, courtesy of Photofest; 86: Elvis Presley, courtesy of

Presley, courtesy of Everett Collection; 87: Keith Richards and Mick Jagger © Wide World Photo; 88: Alain Delon, courtesy of Photofest; 90: Marlon Brando in *The Wild One*, courtesy of Everett Collection; 91: Dennis Hopper and James Dean in *Rebel Without A Cause*, courtesy of Everett Collection; 93: Richard Gere, courtesy of Photofest; 93: John Travolta in *Urban Cowboy*, courtesy of Photofest; 95: Peter Fonda in *Easy Rider*, courtesy of Everett Collection; 98: Steve McQueen © William Claxton; 101: Kirk Douglas and Peter Sellers, courtesy of Everett Collection; 102: Sylvester Stallone in *F.I.S.T.* © United Artists Corporation; 103: Burt Lancaster in *From Here To Eternity*, courtesy of Everett Collection; 103: Woody Allen © Corbis; 103: David Hemmings © Letterpress; 104: Fred Astaire © John Engstead, courtesy of MPTV; 104: James Stewart © Ted Allan, courtesy of MPTV; 108: Douglas Fairbanks Jr., courtesy of Everett Collection; 110: Douglas Fairbanks J., courtesy of Everett Collection; 112: Sean Penn in *Fast Times At Ridgemont High*, courtesy of Everett Collection; 112: Andy Garcia in *Dead Again*, courtesy of Everett Collection; 113: Humphrey Bogart, courtesy of Everett Collection; 113: Paul Newman © Corbis; 113: Nat King Cole, courtesy of MPTV; 113: Jean-Paul Belmondo in *Breathless*, courtesy of Everett Collection; 115: Frank Sinatra and Ava Gardner, courtesy of Everett Collection; 116: Gary Cooper, courtesy of Everett Collection; 120: Clark Gable © Clarence T. Bull, courtesy of MPTV; 120: Edward Fox in *The Day of the Jackel*, courtesy of Everett Collection; 121: Robert Redford in *The Great Gatsby*, courtesy of Everett Collection; 121: David Hemmings, courtesy of Photofest; 123: Humphrey Bogart, courtesy of Photofest; 124: Tyrone Power, courtesy of Everett Collection; 125: John Huston, courtesy of Photofest; 126: Humphrey Bogart, courtesy of Everett Collection; 127: Clint Eastwood in *Dirty Harry* © Douglas Jones; 128: Robert DeNiro in *Casino*, courtesy of Photofest; 134: Tyrone Power, courtesy of Everett Collection; 136-137: Jean-Paul Belmondo and Jean Seberg in *Breathless*, courtesy of Everett Collection; 139: Humphrey Bogart © Corbis; 140: Johnny Depp in *Blow* © Loney Sebastian, courtesy of MPTV; 141: Robert Redford in *The Great Gatsby*, courtesy of Photofest; 143: Gary Cooper, courtesy of Everett Collection; 144: Douglas Fairbanks Jr. in *Stella Dallas*, courtesy of Everett Collection; 148-149: Harry Belafonte in *Island in the Sun*, courtesy of Everett Collection; 151: Al Pacino in *Scarface*, courtesy of Everett Collection; 152: Ethan Hawke in *Gattaca*, courtesy of Everett Collection; 153: Quentin Tarantino in *Reservoir Dogs*, courtesy of Collection Christophe L; 153: Harvey Keitel, Tim Roth, Michael Madsen, Steve Buscemi, Edward Bunker and Quentin Tarantino in *Reservoir Dogs*, courtesy of Collection Christophe L; 155: Clint Eastwood, courtesy of Photofest; 156: Orson Welles in *The Lady from Shanghai*, courtesy of Photofest; 156: Keanu Reeves in *The Matrix*, courtesy of Photofest; 157: Sean Penn in *State of Grace*, courtesy of Everett Collection; 162: James Dean © Bob Willoughby; 163: Richard Roundtree in *Shaft*, courtesy of Everett Collection; 164-165: John Lennon, George Harrison, Ringo Starr and Paul McCartney in *A Hard Day's Night*, courtesy of Everett Collection

ACKNOWLEDGMENTS·168

Acknowledgments

Elliot Raban and Anthony T. Kirby at Peter Elliot were exceptionally generous with clothes and ideas for this book. The good people at Bergdorf Goodman men's store and Hugo Boss also lent clothes and ideas.

Joan Moore and Jessica Dolan at the Everett Collection made this project a pleasure to work on. Their enthusiasm, which often exceeded even my own, constantly reminded me why I had embarked on it in the first place.

Ellen Nidy deserves special thanks for coming into the project late and bearing up under great pressures. Her unfailing good humor literally made this book possible.